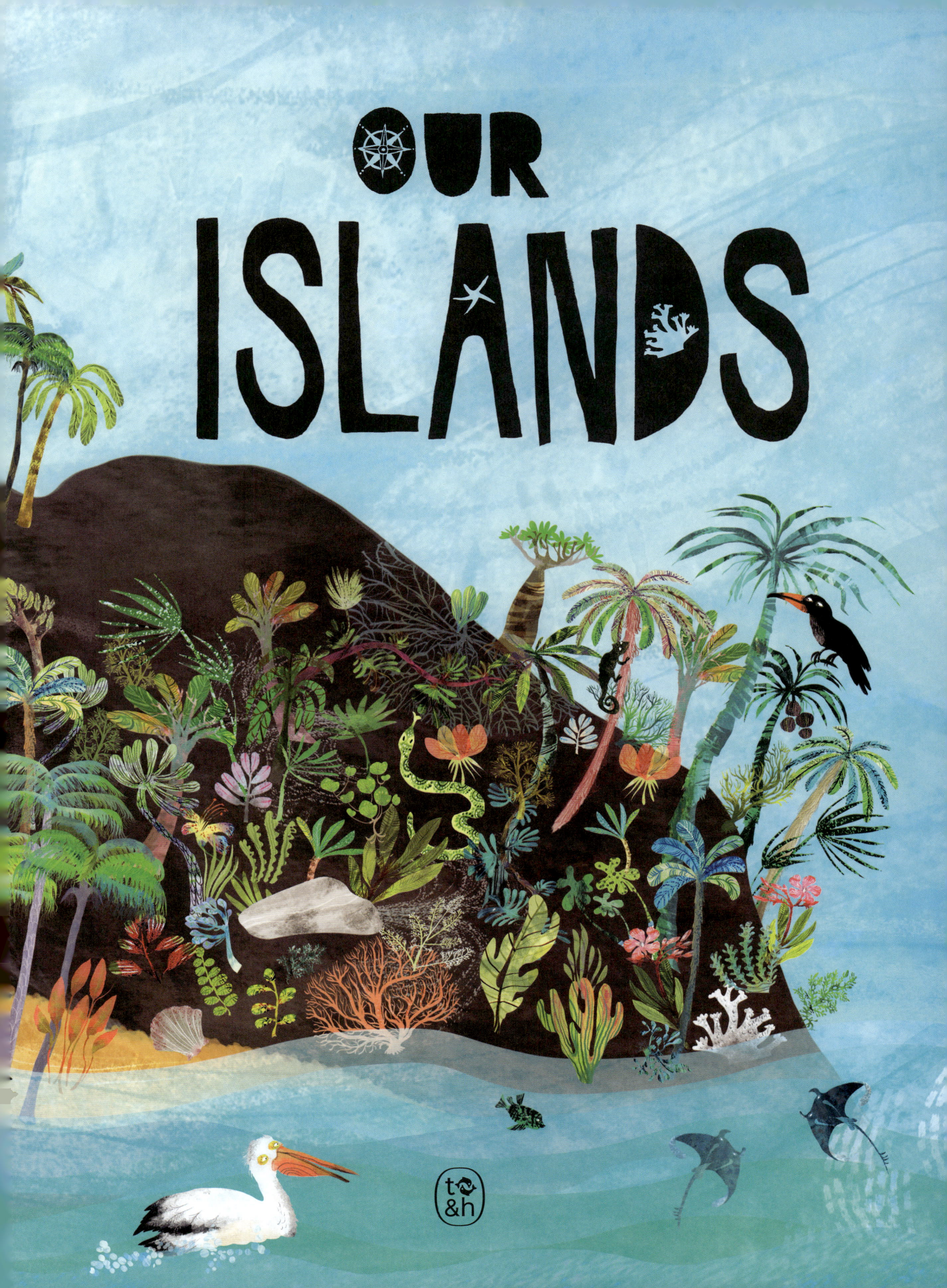

CONTENTS

What is an island?	6
Trinidad	8
Easter Island	10
Zanzibar	12
Types of island	14
Socotra	16
Ross Island	18
Hawai'i	20
Madagascar	22
People and islands	24
St Kilda	26

Borneo	28
Crete	30
Island legends	32
K'gari	34
Svalbard	36
Galápagos Islands	38
Shipwrecked!	40
Where in the world?	42
Did you find...	44
Island words	46
Index	47

WHAT IS AN ISLAND?

An island is a piece of land completely surrounded by water. If you want to travel to any of the islands in this book, you'll have to fly or take a boat.

How many islands are there?
No one knows exactly. There are over 600,000 islands but lots of little ones haven't been counted yet...and some are still waiting to be discovered!

Which is the biggest?
Greenland is the world's largest island. It measures over 2 million square kilometres, but that's still almost 4 times smaller than Australia, the smallest continent.

Do you live on an island?
A lot of countries are islands. Some, like Japan or the Philippines, are made up of a group of islands, called an archipelago.

What makes islands special?
Many islands are home to animals and plants found nowhere else on Earth.

Can islands disappear?
Islands can shrink or sink for different reasons. Global warming is melting polar ice and causing oceans to expand and rise. This is putting some islands in danger of being completely flooded.

DID YOU KNOW?
If every island in the ocean was joined together into one, it would be about the size of Canada.

TRINIDAD

How many birds live here?
Almost 500 different species of birds have been found in Trinidad, including the dazzling scarlet ibis and many different hummingbirds.

Welcome to carnival!
Once a year, the streets fill with celebration, parades, music and people in colourful costumes.

GULF OF PARIA

Dino-turtles
Leatherback turtles are ancient. They have hardly changed since the days of the dinosaurs, over 100 million years ago.

CARIBBEAN SEA

Bat mountain
Mount Tamana contains a huge network of caves, which are home to 11 species of bats.

Munching manatees
Manatees spend up to 8 hours a day eating underwater plants.

Sea swamps
Mangroves are trees that grow in salty water. Trinidad's mangrove swamps are home to lots of wildlife, including caimans and manatees.

NORTH ATLANTIC OCEAN

Land of giants
The island is famous for its huge stone figures, called moai. More than 900 were created by Rapa Nui people between 400 and 1,000 years ago.

A home for horses
There are thousands of horses on the island. They were brought here by humans and now roam free.

Where are all the trees?
The forests that once covered the island were all destroyed by humans and rats that came from overseas.

SOUTH PACIFIC OCEAN

EASTER ISLAND

How did the island get its name?
Dutch explorers named the island when they arrived on Easter Sunday in 1722. But the Rapa Nui people had arrived hundreds of years earlier. Local people today call the island Rapa Nui.

Plenty of fish
There isn't much wildlife on the island itself, but in the surrounding waters there are 142 ocean species that are found nowhere else.

DID YOU KNOW?
It's thought that the moai represented important people who had died.

ZANZIBAR

What is the land made of?
This is Zanzibar's main island, Unguja. Much of its land is made of coral reef that has been fossilised, which means turned into rock over millions of years.

Underwater farming
Seaweed farmers hang seaweed on ropes in the water until they grow big enough to harvest.

Wind in the trees
Zanzibar red colobus monkeys eat leaves and unripe fruit that makes them very gassy! They spend a lot of time napping and farting in the trees.

Spice island
Zanzibar is famous for growing lots of cooking spices, including cinnamon, cloves, black pepper and nutmeg.

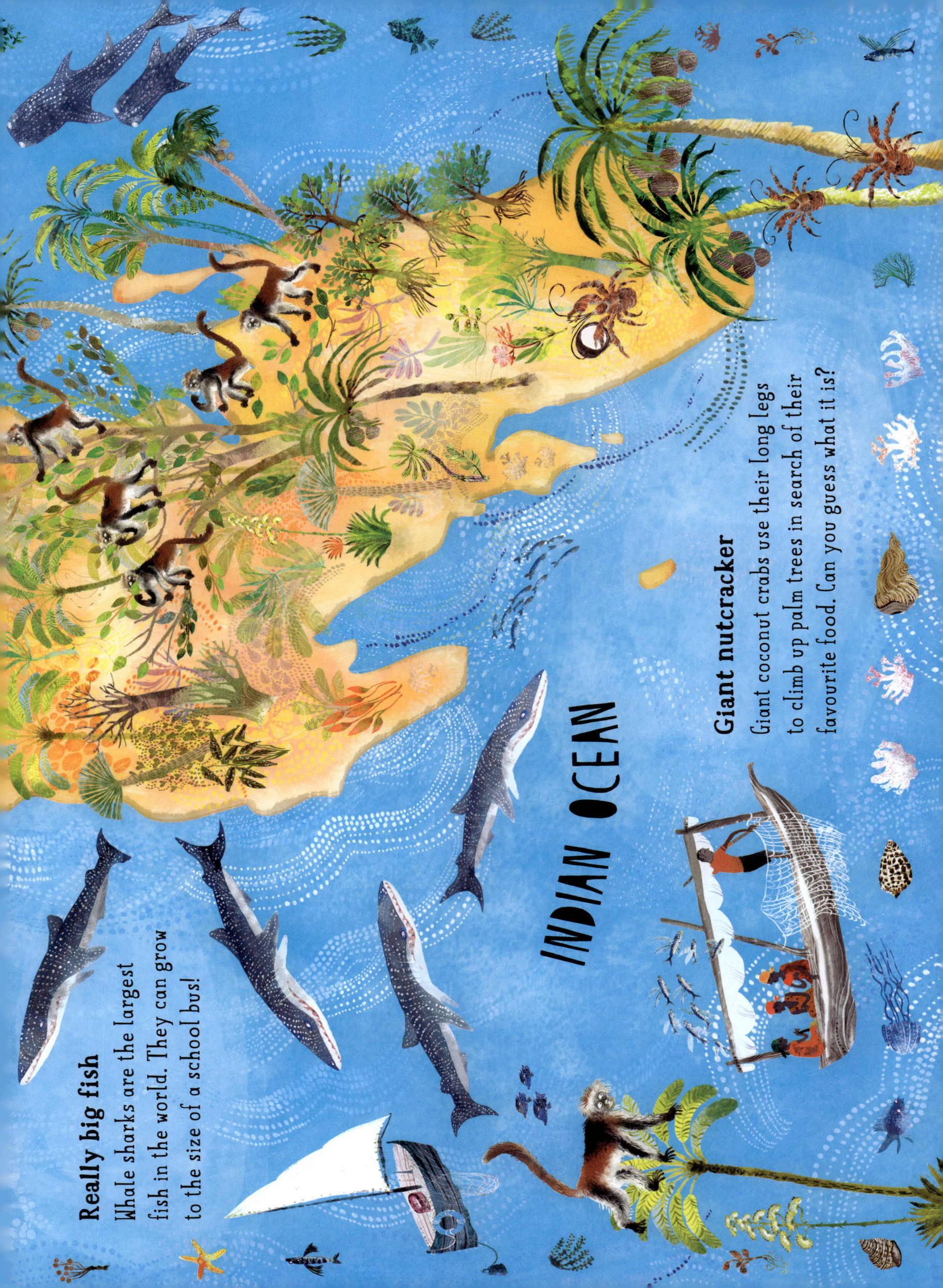

Giant nutcracker
Giant coconut crabs use their long legs to climb up palm trees in search of their favourite food. Can you guess what it is?

INDIAN OCEAN

Really big fish
Whale sharks are the largest fish in the world. They can grow to the size of a school bus!

TYPES OF ISLAND

How are islands made?

Most islands are created naturally over a very long period of time. Here are some different ways islands can form.

CONTINENTAL ISLANDS

These islands were once part of a continent but became separated over time. Some form as slow movements of the Earth's crust split chunks of land apart. Others form when rising seas flood low land, leaving higher areas cut off.

OCEANIC ISLANDS

Also known as 'volcanic islands', these islands are created when lava from an erupting underwater volcano builds up in layers to form a mountain under the sea. Eventually it rises above the surface and becomes an island.

BARRIER ISLANDS

These long, thin islands are found close to coasts and are made of sand that has been moved into place by wind, waves and tides over time. They protect the coast by blocking incoming storms.

CORAL ISLANDS

These are low islands made from coral reefs.

ARTIFICAL ISLANDS

Some islands are made by humans rather than nature. They are sometimes made in the shape of other things, like palm trees.

Ancient shopping
Many ancient people, including the Romans, used to sail here to buy precious incense, resins and medicines made from plants on the island.

ARABIAN SEA

Upside-down trees
Dragon's blood trees suck precious water from the air through their leaves. If you cut their bark they ooze red resin.

INDIAN OCEAN

Tree-climbing snails
There are 96 types of snail on Socotra and most of them are found nowhere else. They often hang out on tree trunks to escape the heat.

ROSS ISLAND

Would a sneeze freeze here?
This snowy wonderland in Antarctica is one of the coldest islands on Earth. It's so cold that your snot would freeze if you sneezed!

ROSS SEA

Stop thief!
Thousands of Adélie penguins live here. The male penguins build nests out of pebbles to attract females. Sometimes they steal stones from other nests.

Polar predators
Leopard seals are tough predators. They hunt animals including fish, penguins and even other seals. But they are no match for killer whales!

SOUTHERN OCEAN

Iceberg ahead!
An iceberg is a large, floating island of ice that has broken off from an ice sheet or glacier. In 2000, one iceberg that broke off from the Ross Ice Shelf was larger than Jamaica!

Fire and ice
Mount Erebus is the most active volcano in Antarctica. Steaming vents in its sides have created massive ice towers and caves.

ROSS ICE SHELF

DID YOU KNOW?
Ross Island is connected to mainland Antarctica by a giant, floating sheet of ice about the size of France, called the Ross Ice Shelf.

19

HAWAI'I

Which volcano is the busiest?
Hawai'i – also known as the Big Island – is home to five volcanoes, including Kīlauea, one of the world's most active volcanoes, which often erupts several times a year.

Surf's up!
The Hawaiian Islands are the birthplace of modern surfing. Some of the biggest and best waves for surfing are found here.

Flower feeders
Hawaiian honeycreepers are little birds with specially shaped beaks for drinking nectar from their favourite flowers.

PACIFIC OCEAN

Blooming beautiful
The yellow hibiscus is the state flower of Hawai'i. Sadly, this precious plant is now endangered.

Rivers of fire
Kīpukas are areas of land surrounded by lava flows from volcanoes. Kīpukas are like mini islands of their own, with different wildlife on each one.

DID YOU KNOW?
Mauna Kea on Hawai'i is the tallest mountain in the world! It's more than 1 km taller than Mount Everest but over half of it is underwater.

MADAGASCAR

How old is the oldest island?

Madagascar has been separated from all other land for 88 million years. It is the oldest island in the world! Around 90 per cent of its wildlife is found nowhere else on Earth.

Forest of stone

These razor-sharp rocks are called Tsingy. Many animals live happily here because the spiky stones keep predators and humans out!

Ancient giants

Giant baobab trees can live for over 1,000 years! This avenue is all that remains of a once mighty forest.

Land of lemurs
There are over 110 different types of lemur, which are only found on Madagascar. They have big eyes and long tails.

Keep an eye out!
Chameleons can move each of their eyes separately, so they can look in two directions at once. How many chameleons can you spot?

Fly by night
The Madagascan moon moth only flies at night. Its long tails spin to confuse predators, such as bats.

INDIAN OCEAN

PEOPLE AND ISLANDS

Do you live on an island?
Over 730 million people around the world live on islands. Maybe you're one of them! But most of the world's islands are uninhabited, which means no one lives there.

Alien island
Devon Island in Canada is the largest uninhabited island in the world. Its environment is similar to land on Mars, so scientists are using it to prepare for future space missions.

Getting crowded
Îlet-à-Brouée is a tiny island off the coast of Haiti. It is smaller than a football pitch but around 500 people live there, making it one of the most crowded islands in the world.

Island clean up

Nobody lives on Henderson Island in the Pacific Ocean, but that hasn't stopped millions of pieces of plastic washing up there. Our rubbish is damaging island wildlife around the world. But luckily, many people are working to clean it up. You could help by joining a beach clean near you!

Leave it to nature

Some islands are nature reserves, where no one is allowed to live. Cocos Island near Costa Rica was once a popular place for pirates to hide their treasure, but now it is protected so its wildlife can live in peace.

ST KILDA

Where did all the people go?
For over 2,000 years, humans lived on the small, lonely islands of St Kilda. Eventually, it became too hard to live here and all the people left. No one has lived on the islands since 1930 but that doesn't mean they're empty...

Wild sheep
Soay sheep are a small, ancient breed of sheep that used to be kept as farm animals but now live wild on the islands.

Busy birds
Every year, hundreds of thousands of seabirds flock to the steep cliffs of St Kilda to breed, safely away from predators.

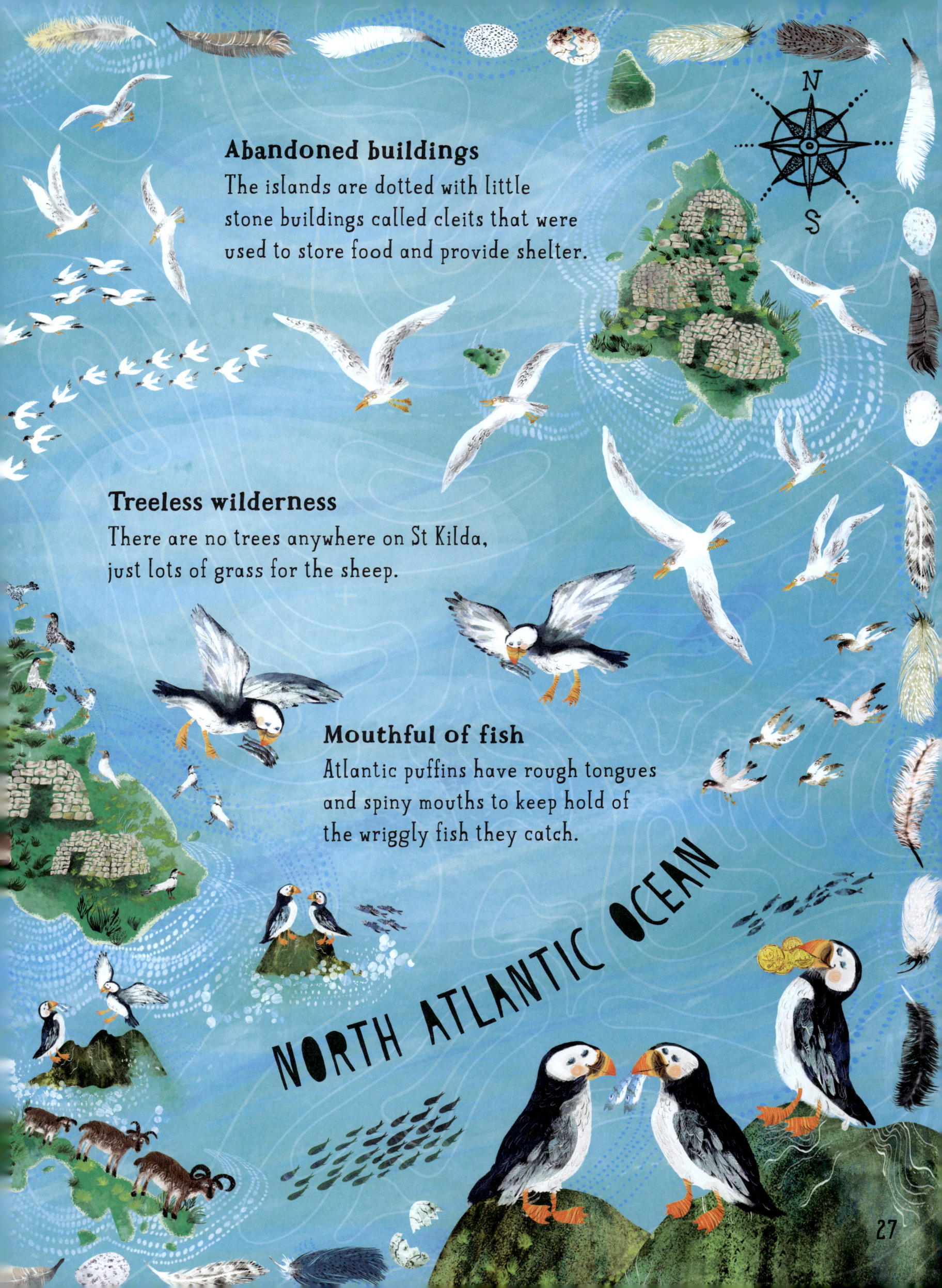

Abandoned buildings
The islands are dotted with little stone buildings called cleits that were used to store food and provide shelter.

Treeless wilderness
There are no trees anywhere on St Kilda, just lots of grass for the sheep.

Mouthful of fish
Atlantic puffins have rough tongues and spiny mouths to keep hold of the wriggly fish they catch.

NORTH ATLANTIC OCEAN

BORNEO

Who's been chopping down trees?

Borneo is famous for its rainforest, which is around 140 million years old. Over half the forest has been destroyed by humans, but luckily lots of people are now working hard to protect it.

SOUTH CHINA SEA

Big but little

The Bornean elephant is the smallest elephant in the world...but it's still the biggest animal on the island.

What's the horn for?

No one knows exactly why the rhinoceros hornbill has a big hollow horn on top of its beak, but some scientists think it could make its call louder.

JAVA SEA

SULU SEA

Hanging about
Bornean orangutans spend almost all their lives up in trees. They even build treetop nests to sleep in.

CELEBES SEA

Is it a bird? Is it a plane?
No, it's a frog! Wallace's flying frog uses its big, webbed feet to glide from tree to tree.

Why the long tongue?
The sun bear is the world's smallest bear. It has a super-long tongue for slurping up insects and honey.

PACIFIC OCEAN

Ancient times
The Minoan people ruled Crete from around 3,000 BCE to 1,100 BCE. Ruins from their grand palaces and cities have been found all over the island, along with artefacts including beautiful pottery.

Monsters and mazes
A famous myth about a giant maze called a labyrinth and a bull-headed monster known as the minotaur is set on Crete. A maze-like ruin was discovered in 2024. Was it a real labyrinth?

MEDITERRANEAN SEA

ISLAND LEGENDS

Do you want to hear some stories?

Many islands have their own legends that have been told for centuries by the Indigenous people who live there. Some of these tales are about how the islands were made.

A good throw!

According to an ancient Greek myth, the island of Santorini grew up from the sea when Euphemus, son of the sea god Poseidon, threw a clump of earth into the water.

Fishing for islands

Māui is a hero who appears in the myths of many Polynesian islands, from Hawai'i all the way to New Zealand. In one legend, he pulls a giant fish from the sea with a magical hook, and that fish became the North Island of New Zealand.

Scottish sea monster

The Scottish island of Orkney has a tale about a giant sea monster called the Stoor Worm, who destroyed wildlife and humans with its poisonous breath. When a brave young farmer defeated the Stoor Worm, its teeth fell out and became the islands of Orkney, Shetland and the Faroes, and its body curled up to became Iceland.

Lucky dip

In the Japanese creation story, two gods called Izanagi and Izanami dipped a spear into the sea. When they pulled it out again, the water that dripped off the spear became the first island of Japan.

K'GARI

What's its name again?
The Butchulla people who have lived on this Australian island for thousands of years called it K'gari, but Europeans who came here 200 years ago renamed it 'Fraser Island'. In 2023, out of respect for the Butchulla people, K'gari officially got its name back.

Mighty big beach
K'gari is the largest island in the world made entirely of sand. It is covered in huge sand dunes that reach up to 240 metres high.

Sandy roots
K'gari is the only place on Earth where tall rainforests grow in sand.

CORAL SEA

SOUTH PACIFIC OCEAN

Island in flames

As climate change makes our planet hotter and drier, K'gari is more at risk of fires, which put local wildlife in danger. In 2020, a giant fire burned over half of the island.

Shipwrecked

The ship SS Maheno washed ashore during a big storm in 1935. Its wreck is still there today.

DID YOU KNOW?

K'gari is pronounced 'gurri', with a silent 'K' and means 'paradise' in the Butchulla language.

Wild dogs

Dingoes are a type of wild dog found across Australia. Dingoes on K'gari are the purest of all as there are no pet dogs to mix with.

SVALBARD

How far to the North Pole?
This Arctic archipelago is less than 3 hours away from the North Pole by plane. More than half of Svalbard is covered in ice, including huge frozen rivers called glaciers.

Colour changers
Arctic foxes change from brown in summer to pure white in winter to blend in with their snowy surroundings.

Frozen seeds
It's too cold for trees to grow here, but the Svalbard Global Seed Vault stores millions of seeds from all over the planet.

GREENLAND SEA

DID YOU KNOW?
From mid-November to the end of January, Svalbard is plunged into polar night. This means the sun never rises and stars shine during the day.

Unicorn of the sea
The male narwhal's long spiral horn isn't actually a horn at all. It's a giant tooth, like an elephant's tusk.

BARENTS SEA

Wondrous whales
The beluga whale's white skin is good camouflage against ice in the Arctic Ocean.

ARCTIC OCEAN

37

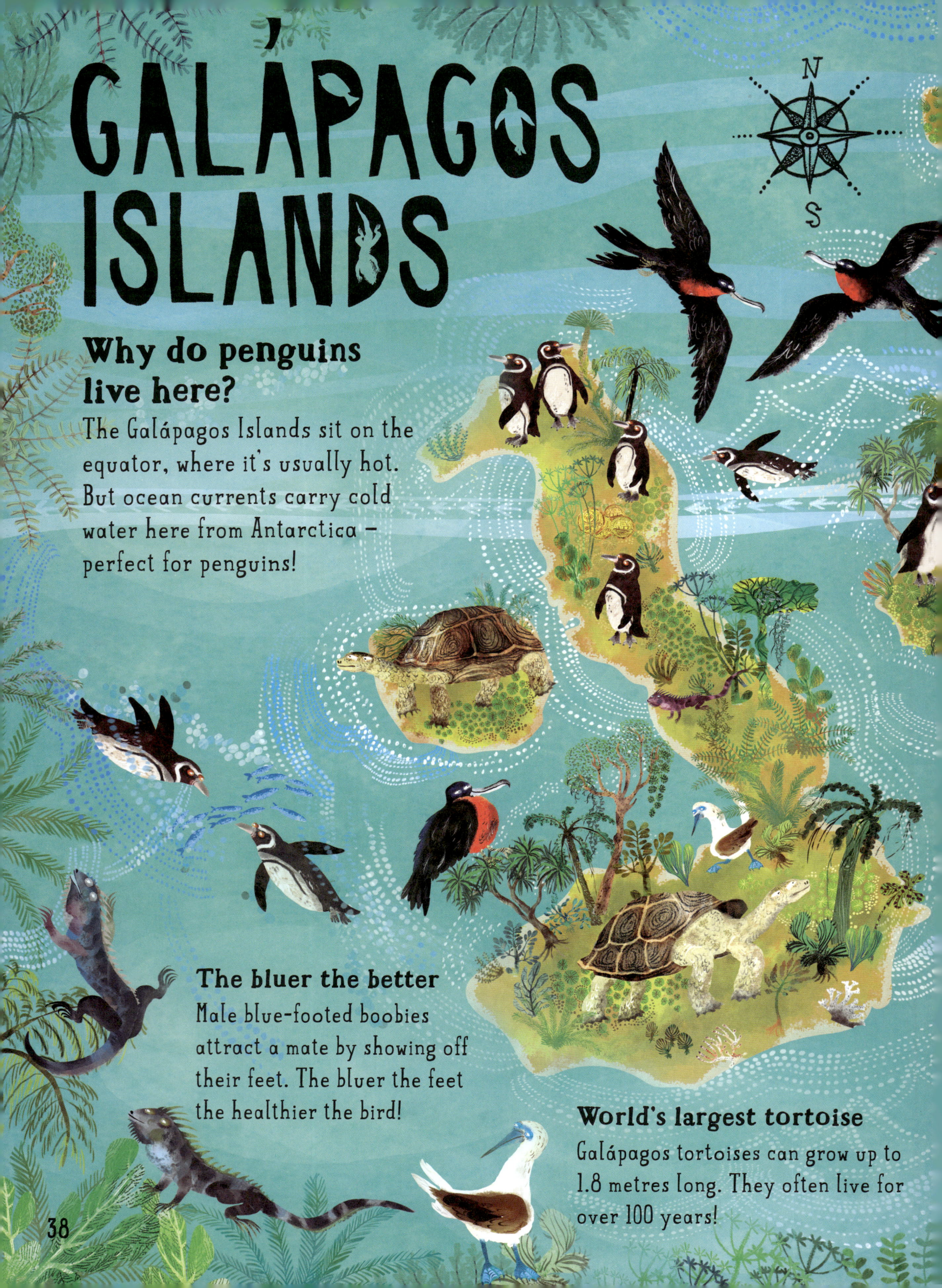

GALÁPAGOS ISLANDS

Why do penguins live here?
The Galápagos Islands sit on the equator, where it's usually hot. But ocean currents carry cold water here from Antarctica – perfect for penguins!

The bluer the better
Male blue-footed boobies attract a mate by showing off their feet. The bluer the feet the healthier the bird!

World's largest tortoise
Galápagos tortoises can grow up to 1.8 metres long. They often live for over 100 years!

Salty sneezes

Marine iguanas swim around the islands eating algae and seaweed. To stop them slurping up too much salt from the water, they sneeze it out through their nostrils. Bless you!

It's a small world

Famous scientist and explorer Charles Darwin called this archipelago 'a little world within itself' because he found different types of animals on each of the islands.

EQUATOR

Shark spotting

Over 30 types of shark are found around these islands, including whale sharks, hammerheads and tiger sharks. How many can you spot?

PACIFIC OCEAN

SHIPWRECKED

Oh no! You've been stranded on a desert island. What should you do next?

Make a fire
A fire will provide warmth, light and somewhere to boil water and cook food.

Build a shelter
Collect logs, branches and big leaves to build a shelter.

Collect drinking water
Collect rainwater in large leaves or bottles that have washed to shore. Water collected from rivers or lakes on the island must be boiled to make it safe to drink.

Find food
Search for edible fruits, nuts and seeds. You could also try to catch fish or birds.

Call for help
Write 'HELP' or 'SOS' in large letters on the beach. You could also try throwing damp logs on a fire to send a smoke signal, or try a message in a bottle!

WHERE IN THE WORLD?

Hawai'i
Location: Pacific Ocean
Island type: Oceanic

Galápagos Islands
Location: Pacific Ocean
Island type: Oceanic

Easter Island
Location: South Pacific Ocean
Island type: Oceanic

Trinidad
Location: North Atlantic Ocean
Island type: Continental

Madagascar
Location: Indian Ocean
Island type: Continental

Svalbard
Location: Arctic Ocean
Island type: Oceanic

St Kilda
Location: North Atlantic Ocean
Island type: Oceanic

Crete
Location: Mediterranean Sea
Island type: Oceanic

Socotra
Location: Indian Ocean
Island type: Continental

Borneo
Location: Pacific Ocean
Island type: Continental

K'gari
Location: South Pacific Ocean
Island type: Barrier

Ross Island
Location: Southern Ocean
Island type: Oceanic

Zanzibar
Location: Indian Ocean
Island type: Oceanic

43

DID YOU FIND...

...the 10 piles of pirate treasure hidden around the islands? Did you know that faraway islands made great places for swashbuckling pirates to hide out from the law? Madagascar was a popular pirate hangout in the 17th and 18th centuries.

8-9 Trinidad

10-11 Easter Island

16-17 Socotra

18-19 Ross Island

44

20–21 Hawai'i

26–27 St Kilda

28–29 Borneo

30–31 Crete

36–37 Svalbard

38–39 Galápagos Islands

45

ISLAND WORDS

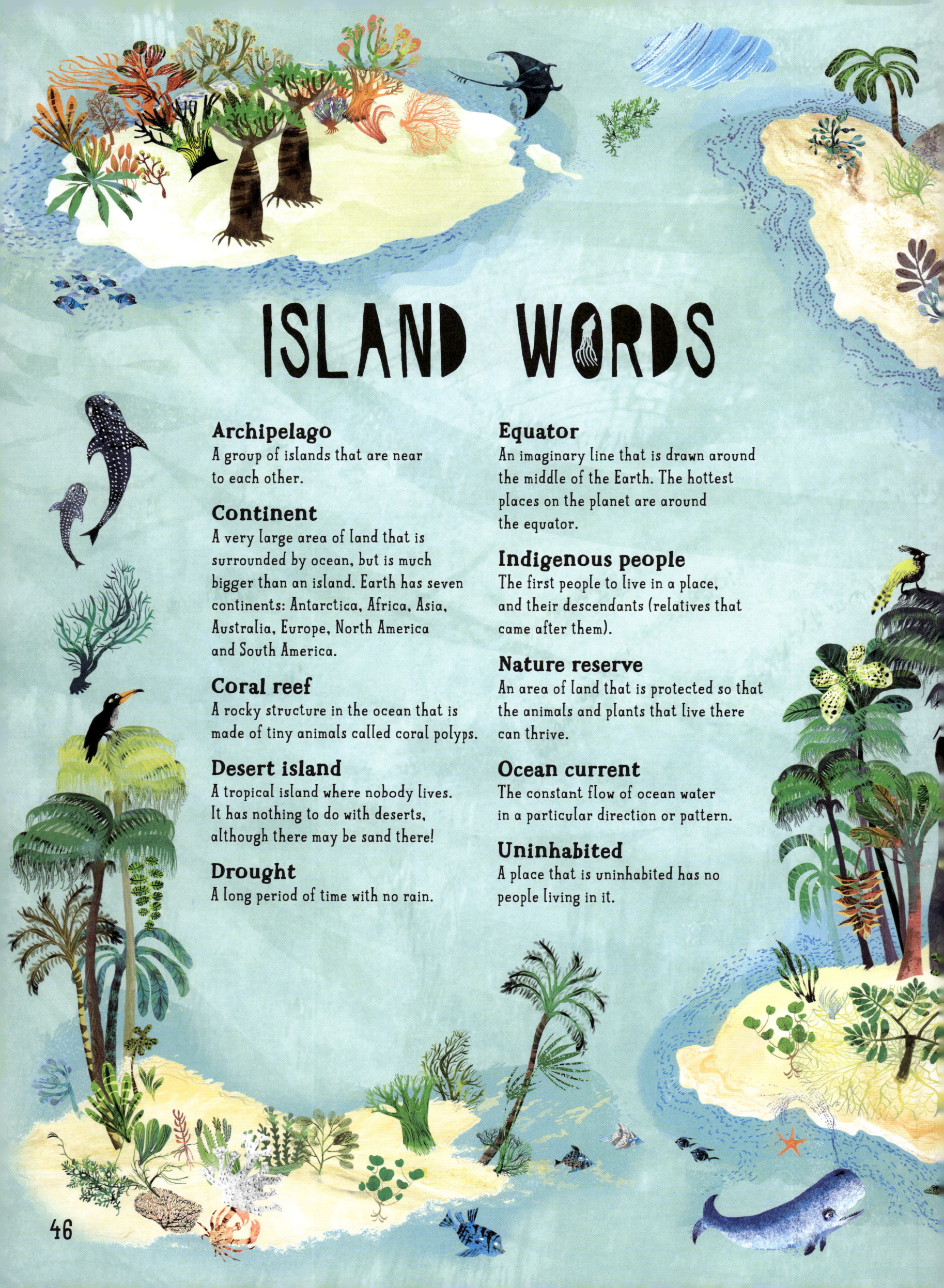

Archipelago
A group of islands that are near to each other.

Continent
A very large area of land that is surrounded by ocean, but is much bigger than an island. Earth has seven continents: Antarctica, Africa, Asia, Australia, Europe, North America and South America.

Coral reef
A rocky structure in the ocean that is made of tiny animals called coral polyps.

Desert island
A tropical island where nobody lives. It has nothing to do with deserts, although there may be sand there!

Drought
A long period of time with no rain.

Equator
An imaginary line that is drawn around the middle of the Earth. The hottest places on the planet are around the equator.

Indigenous people
The first people to live in a place, and their descendants (relatives that came after them).

Nature reserve
An area of land that is protected so that the animals and plants that live there can thrive.

Ocean current
The constant flow of ocean water in a particular direction or pattern.

Uninhabited
A place that is uninhabited has no people living in it.

INDEX

A
Antarctica 18-19
archipelago 7, 36, 39, 46
Arctic 36-37, 43
Australia 6, 34-35

B
Borneo 28-29
Butchulla people 34

C
climate change 25
Cocos Island 25
continent 6, 14, 46
coral reef 12, 15, 46
Crete 30-31

D
desert island 16-17, 40-41, 46
Devon Island 24
droughts 17, 46

E
Easter Island 10-11
equator 38-39, 46

F
floods 7, 14

G
Galápagos Islands 38-39
glaciers 19, 36
global warming 7

H
Hawai'i 20-21
Henderson Island 25

I
icebergs 19
Ilet a Brouee 24

J
Japan 7, 33

K
K'gari 34-35

M
Madagascar 22-23
Minoan people 31
mountains 9, 14, 21
myths 30, 31, 32-33

N
nature reserves 25, 46
New Zealand 32

O
ocean currents 38, 46
Orkney 33

P
Philippines 7
pirates 25, 44
Polynesia 32

R
rainforest 28, 34
Rapa Nui people 10, 11
Ross Island 18-19

S
sand dunes 34
Santorini 32
shipwreck 35, 40-41
Socotra 16-17
St Kilda 26-27
Svalbard 36-37

T
Trinidad 8-9

uninhabited islands 24, 25, 26-27, 46

U
Unguja 12-13

V
volcanoes 14, 19, 20, 21

Z
Zanzibar 12-13

47

To my wonderful niece Noya, with love.

First published in the United Kingdom in 2025 by
Thames and Hudson Ltd, 6-24 Britannia Street, London WC1X 9JD

Our Islands © 2025 Yuval Zommer
Consultancy by Barbara Taylor

All Rights Reserved. No part of this publication may be reproduced or transmitted in any form or by any means, electronic or mechanical, including photocopy, recording or any other information storage and retrieval system, without prior permission in writing from the publisher.

EU Authorized Representative: Interart S.A.R.L.
19 rue Charles Auray, 93500 Pantin, Paris, France
productsafety@thameshudson.co.uk
interart.fr

A CIP catalogue record for this book is available from the British Library

ISBN 978-0-500-65368-5

01

Printed and bound in China
by Shenzhen C&C Offset Printing Co. Ltd.

Be the first to know about our new releases, exclusive content and author events by visiting
thamesandhudson.com
thamesandhudsonusa.com
thamesandhudson.com.au

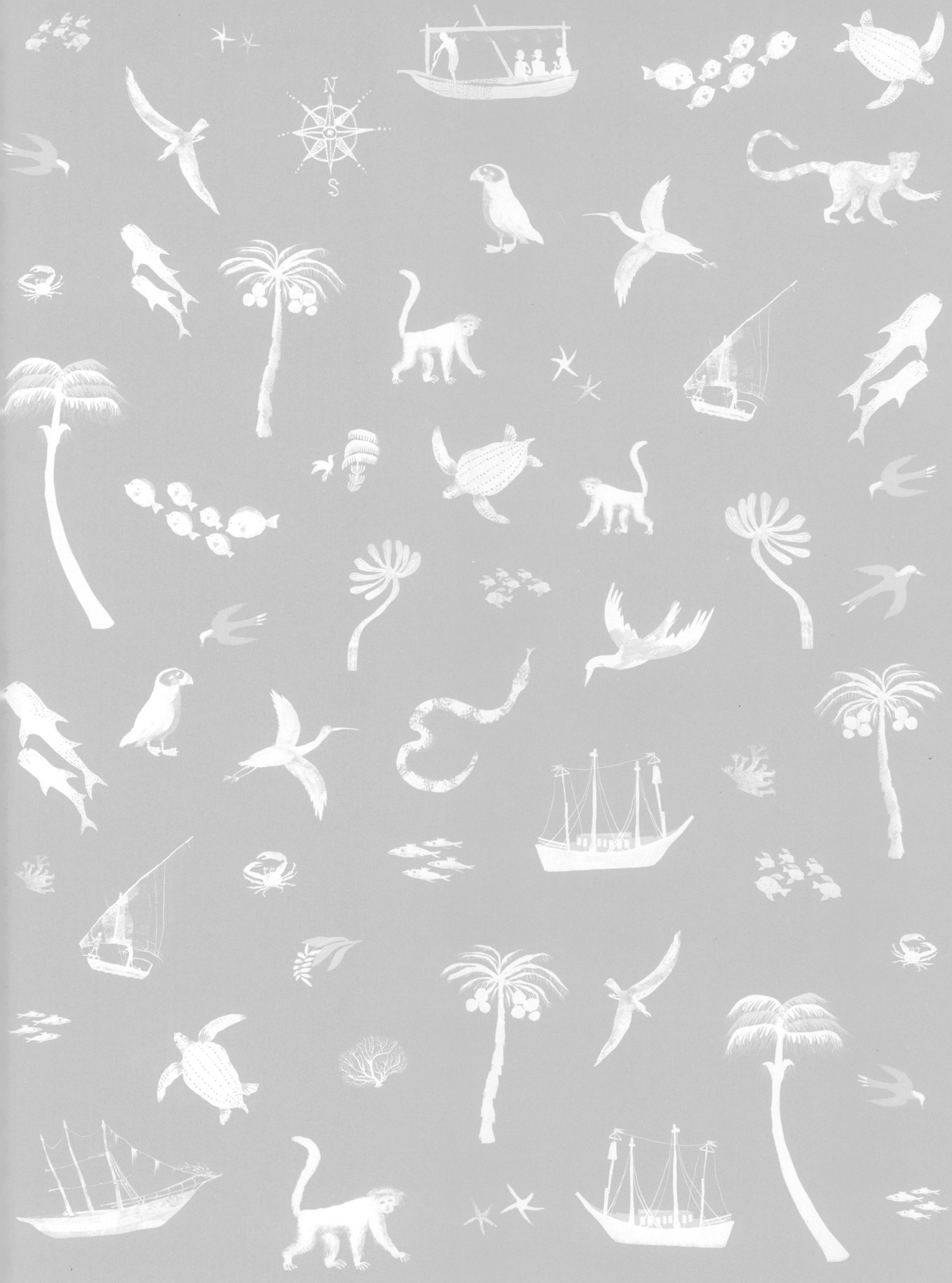
N
S

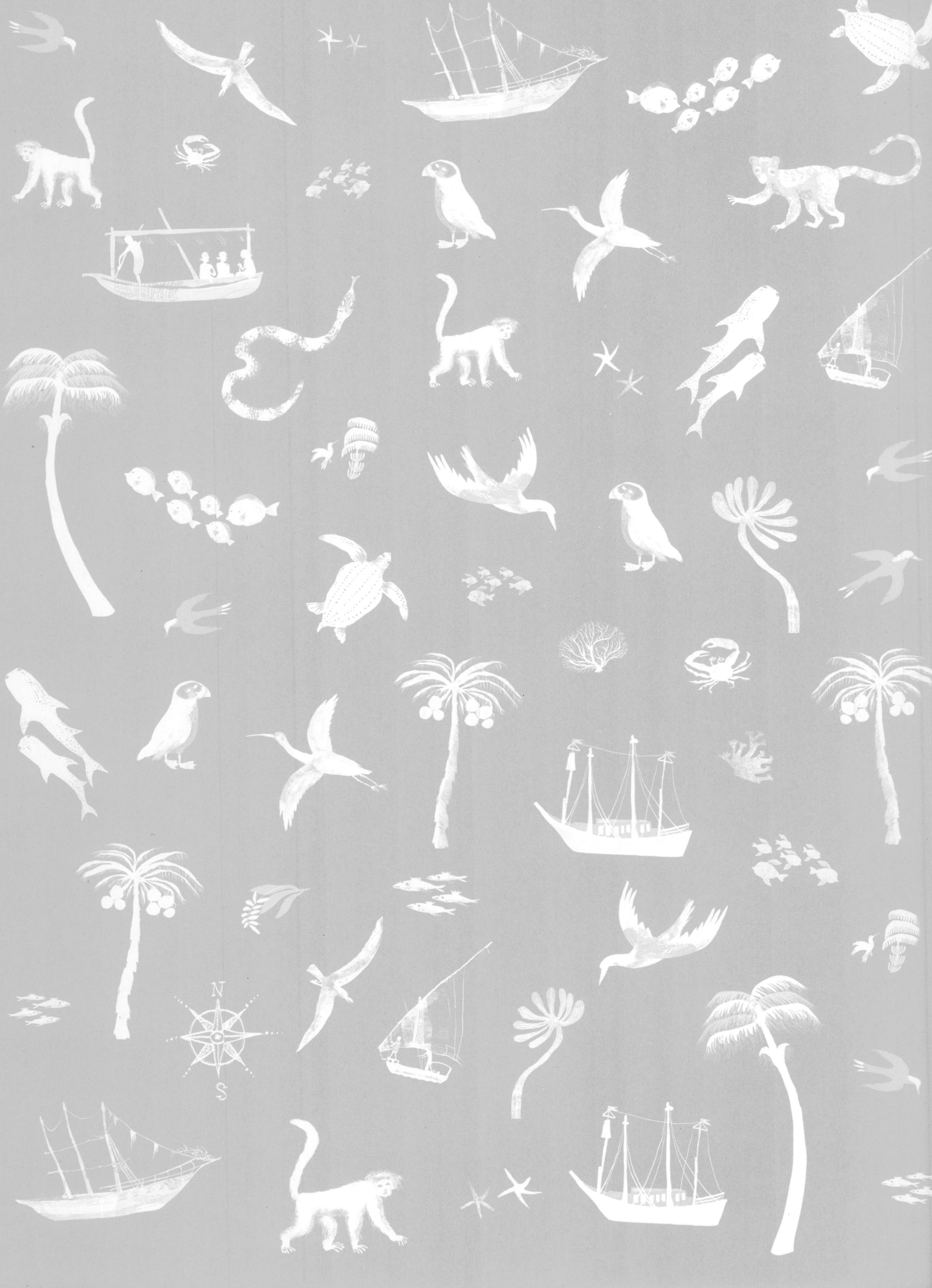
N
S